DAVID:

CHERISHED BY GOD

A Mighty Man In Battle

J.T Hays

TABLE OF CONTENTS

INTRODUCTION

When you think of the Bible character David, what comes to mind? Goliath, the Philistine giant, was defeated by him. Or because of King Saul's anger for him, which led him to flee into the wilderness? His sin with Bath-Sheba, and the consequence that followed it? Perhaps his inspired poetry is found in the book of Psalms in the Bible?

When we first encounter David, he is a young shepherd kid tasked with caring for his father's flock of sheep. This work most certainly required him to spend long, lonely days and nights out in the field. David's family dwelt in Bethlehem, a small town on the ridge's crest and slopes in Judah's hills. Grain crops were abundant in the stony fields surrounding Bethlehem. The gentler slopes and valleys were covered in orchards, olive

3

groves, and vineyards. The uncultivated uplands were most likely used for pasture in David's day. The wilderness of Judah lay beyond.

Shepherding was, for the most part, a peaceful and solitary profession. David, on the other hand, did not allow himself to become bored. The serene stillness, on the other hand, provided him with ample opportunity for meditation. Some of David's psalms feature comments from his youth, which seems to be the case. Was it in his moments of isolation that he studied man's role in the universe and the wonders of the heavens—the sun, moon, and stars?

David's life was full of opportunities, achievements, and setbacks. But what the prophet Samuel said about David draws us to him beyond all else: he will prove to be "a man-pleasing to God's heart." —1 Samuel 13:14. When David was still a child, Samuel's prophecy came true. Wouldn't it be nice to be described as someone pleasing to Jehovah's heart? So, what can you learn from David's life, particularly his early years, to help you become such a person? Let's see what happens.

CHAPTER ONE
THEY ASKED FOR A HUMAN KING.

The country of Israel was unique among the nations of the world for four centuries after they departed Egypt. It was ruled by God and had no human king. From the time of Judge Joshua until the 356 years that his assigned judges dispense justice and save Israel from their adversaries, God reigns as the true King, the heavenly King of Israel. They were ruled by his laws, which were inextricably linked to his power. Overseers were appointed to ensure that his will was carried out for the greater good of the people. They prospered as long as they obeyed their invisible Ruler. Rather than being satisfied with this holy King, they demanded a human ruler.

"Give us a king," they say. They called out to Samuel, the prophet. (8:6) (1 Samuel) They aspired to be like the other nations, with a human ruler who would lead them into battle and whose splendor and majesty they could witness. It wasn't that they didn't have a king; they did, in the form of God himself. He was the King of the nation. Even visible governmental officials, and the judges, whom God established to serve his people, were given to them. However, because there was no hereditary line of kings. Samuel's sons could not have envisioned how far their greed and selfishness would spread. The Israelites' desire for a visible royal commander-in-chief may have been influenced by the threat of the Philistine and Ammonite attacks. As a nation and as individuals, they thereby demonstrated a lack of faith in God's capacity to protect, lead, and provide for them.

"It is not you whom they have rejected, but it is I whom they have rejected from becoming king over them," God said in response to Samuel's prayer. —1 Samuel 8:4–7. Samuel then cautioned them about the oppression they would face if a human ruler reigned over them, but they said, "No, but a king will rule over us." And we, like all other nations, must become, and our king must judge us.

The Appointment Of Israel's First King

Samuel was told by God that Saul will be the first king. Samuel crowned Saul as king by pouring oil over his head when he visited Samuel in Ramah. Saul has great qualities and had received God's blessing. He also recognized God's power. The Israelites and their king sustained success. Samuel however urged them to be obedient to God because it will mean life for them.

Obedience was and continues to be, the key to receiving God's blessing. God blesses those who obey his commands. But what if they reject God's commands?

David Replaces Saul After He Is Rejected

Saul was the first king of ancient Israel. Despite being chosen by the true God, Saul eventually rebelled.

What mistakes did Saul make? Is it possible that he might have averted them? Saul made a critical miscalculation during a war against the Amalekites. Rather than following God's order to kill the hostile Amalekites and their belongings, Saul captured their king and preserved their best livestock. What occurred when Samuel confronted Saul about this?

Saul attempted to divert culpability by claiming that the people were kind enough to sacrifice the best of the flock and herd to God. Whether or not Saul planned to sacrifice the animals, he had disobeyed God. Saul had disobeyed God, according to God's prophet. "God delights more in obedience than burnt offering and sacrifices" Samuel continued. Look! It's better to obey than to make a sacrifice... Because you have rejected Jehovah's word, he has removed you from the throne." 1 Samuel 15:15,17:22,23.

When God took away Saul's holy spirit and blessing, "an evil spirit" took control of Israel's first king. Saul's attitude toward David—a man to whom God would ultimately bestow the throne—became marked by hatred and jealousy.

God made it clear to Samuel that he had rejected Saul from ruling as king over Israel and asked him to fill his horn with oil and head out the door. God sent him to Jesse the Bethlehemite to go choose a king among his sons. Jesse summoned his sons when God's prophet came to Bethlehem. Samuel was to appoint one of them as a king. Samuel thought to himself, "This is the," when he saw Eliab, the eldest. "Do not stare at his attractiveness or the height of his stature, for I have rejected him," God instructed Samuel. Because mere man sees what appears to the eyes, but Jehovah sees what the heart is, the way he sees is not the way God sees." Similarly, Abinadab, Shammah, and four of their brothers were rejected by Jehovah.

"Finally," the account says, "Samuel asked Jesse, 'Are these all the boys?'. Jesse confirmed that David had gone to the field to pasture the livestock. —1 Samuel 16:7,11.

'David can't possibly be the one you're looking for,' Jesse appears to imply in his response. David had been assigned the task of looking after the sheep because he was the youngest and least important member of the household. He was, nevertheless, the one whom God had selected. God sees the heart, and he saw something extremely valuable in this young man. God commanded Samuel when Jesse sent for David "Go on, anoint him, for he is the chosen one!". As a result, Samuel took the horn of oil and anointed himself in the presence of his brothers. From that day on, the spirit of Jehovah started to work upon David."

David's age at the time of the incident is unknown. However, Eliab, Abinadab, and Shammah, the three oldest brothers, were serving in Saul's army at the time. The other five might have been too young to accompany them. It's possible that none of them were yet 20 years old, the minimum age for joining the Israeli army. In any case, God chose David when he was very young. David, on the other hand, appears to have been spiritually inclined from the start. He had a close relationship with God that he built by reflecting on what he had learned about God.

David The Harpist

Music can be used to process emotions, trauma, and loss, but it can also be used as a relaxing or regulating medication for anxiety or dysregulation.

Saul was afflicted by an evil spirit. His attendants reassured him that listening to particular beautifully played instrumental music would cure him of his affliction caused by that demon. The king invited the hero and warrior David, who was famed for his prowess with the harp because the music was supposed to have a curative effect. And anytime God's wicked spirit fell upon Saul, David picked up the lyre and played it with his hand, and Saul was refreshed and well, and the evil spirit left him.

If there is one name that calls to mind biblical music, it is that of David, a great man who lived about 3,000 years ago. Much of what we know about music at the time comes from the Bible's account of David's actions- from his days as a young shepherd through his reign as king and organizer.

Music also played a role in Israel. It was thought to elevate the mind and spiritually empower prophets. Elisha received supernatural inspiration through the sound of a stringed instrument. (2 Kings 3:15) Music was often employed to indicate the start and end of events on the calendar. Two silver trumpets were used to proclaim new moons and festivities. The sound of the horn on Jubilee Day announced slaves' emancipation and the return of forfeited land and buildings to their owners. What joy the poor people must have felt when they heard music heralding the return of their liberty or property!

There must have been some excellent musicians or vocalists among the Israelites. According to an Assyrian bas-relief, King Sennacherib requested a tribute of male and female musicians from King Hezekiah. They appeared to be top-notch performers. But among all the virtuosos, David stood out. David was unique in that he was a musician as well as a poet. He is credited with writing about half of the psalms. He was a shepherd as a child, and the pastoral scenes of Bethlehem fed his sensitive and perceptive intellect. He'd experienced the simple pleasures of listening to babbling brooks and lambs reacting to his voice.

He took up his harp and raised his voice in worship to God because he was moved by the beauty of the "music" in the world around him. What a powerful experience it must have been to hear David's music for Psalm 23! David's harp playing was so magnificent as a young man that he was recommended to King Saul, who took him into his service.

When Saul was overcome with pain and mental turmoil, David came to him and played lovely and soothing refrains on his harp, which soothed the king's heart. Saul's anxiousness subsided as the gloomy ideas that had plagued him faded away. Music, which David adored brought him so much joy.

In many respects, David's divinely inspired compositions excelled. His songs include psalms that are both introspective and pastoral. From praise to the narrative history, from the joys of the grape harvest to the splendor of the palace inauguration, from reminiscences to hope, and from request to entreaty, they cover a wide range of topics. David composed a dirge called "The Bow" after Saul and his son Jonathan died, opening with the words: "The beauty, O Israel, is killed upon your high places." The tone was depressing. David could express a wide spectrum of emotions through both speech and music on his harp. David's energetic attitude made him a fan of upbeat, lively music with a strong rhythm. He leaped and danced with all his might when he took the ark of the covenant up to Zion to commemorate the occasion. According to the Bible, the music must have been highly captivating. Can you picture the scene in your mind? Michal, his wife, expressed her displeasure with him. David, on the other hand, was unconcerned. He adored Jehovah, and the music brought him such joy that he leaped in front of his God.

God gave people music, imbuing them with a love of music and an insatiable desire to express themselves via music, whether through playing an instrument or singing. Music is, above all, a gift from God for the man of faith. The organizing of singing and music in God's house was one of David's legacies. He put Asaph, Heman, and Jeduthun in charge of 4,000 singers and musicians. David put them in touch with 288 professionals who trained and oversaw the remainder of the team. For the three major annual festivities, all 4,000 singers and musicians were present at the temple. Think of the majesty of that magnificent choir!

CHAPTER TWO
DAVID TRIUMPHS OVER GOLIATH.

The Battle Is God's
1 Samuel 17:1–58.

David braced himself against the onrushing army of soldiers. They ran away from the combat line, their eyes wide with terror. What had frightened them so much? David must have overheard them frantically repeating one thing over and over. It was a man's name. And there was the man himself, standing boldly on the valley floor, maybe larger than any man David had ever seen.

Goliath! David could see why the soldiers frightened him—he appeared to be an impossibly large figure. He weighed more than two huge men combined, even without his strong armor. He was, nevertheless, highly armed and a formidable and veteran warrior. Goliath screamed a challenge. Imagine his booming voice taunting Israel's soldiers and its king, Saul, from the hillsides. He challenged anyone to come forward and battle him in single combat to end the conflict!

The Israelites were terrified. King Saul was terrified. David discovered that the situation had been going on for nearly a month! As Goliath's insults continued day after day, the two armies, Philistine and Israelite, remained deadlocked. David was agitated. Imagine Israel's king and his warriors, including three of David's older brothers, trembling in terror! This pagan Goliath, in David's perspective, was doing far more than offending Israel's army; he was insulting Israel's God, Jehovah! But what could David, a mere teenager, do?

And what can we learn from David's faith today?

No One Should Be Fearful Because Of Him.

David frequently returned home to shepherd the sheep while serving Saul, sometimes for long lengths of time. Jesse dispatched David to check on the three oldest sons who were serving in Saul's army during one of these periods. David marched to the Valley of Elah, packed with supplies for his brothers. When he arrived, the two armies were trapped on the s opposite sides of that huge, curved valley, facing one other.

The situation was intolerable to David. How could the armies of Jehovah, the living God, be terrified of a single man—let alone a pagan? Goliath's taunts were seen by David as a direct insult to God. As a result, he began eagerly discussing Goliath's defeat with the army. Eliab, David's older brother, soon learned of David's conversation. He scolded his younger brother, accusing him of simply being there to witness the battle's destruction. "What have I done now?" David responded. "All I asked was a question!" Then he continued confidently speaking about slaying Goliath until his comments were conveyed to Saul. The king demanded that David be brought before him.

"Let no one lose heart because of him," David said to the king about Goliath. Because of Goliath, Saul and his men had lost heart. Perhaps they'd made the common error of comparing themselves to that giant man, imagining how they only came up to his waist or chest. They pictured the armored giant-slaying them with ease. David, on the other hand, did not share this viewpoint. He viewed the situation in a completely different light, as we'll see. As a result, he promised to take on Goliath personally.

Saul objected to David going into the battle against Goliath pointing out that he was just a boy and that Goliath has been a warrior since his youth. Was David a youngster? He was too young to join the army, and he did have a youthful appearance. But David, on the other hand, was already a feared fighter and may have been in his late teens at the time. David assured Saul by telling him about the lion and bear encounter. Is he bragging? No. David was well aware of how he had triumphed in those battles. "God, who protected me from the lion's and bear's claws, he is the one who will rescue me from this Philistine's hand," he said. "Go, and may God be with you," Saul finally said, resigned.

Would you like to have David's faith? David's faith, then, was not merely idealistic or wishful thinking. Because of his knowledge and experience, he had faith in his God. He saw God as a loving Protector and Promise Keeper. We must continue to learn about the God of the Bible if we are to develop such faith. As we put what we've learned into practice, the positive outcomes will enhance our faith.

You Will Be Delivered Into My Hands By God

Saul attempted to equip David with his armor at first. It was made of copper and included a massive hauberk, or shirt of mail, made of overlapping scales, similar to Goliath's. However, when David attempted moving around while wearing that enormous and unwieldy apparatus, he quickly discovered that it was not for him. He had never been trained as a soldier; therefore, he was unaccustomed to wearing armor, particularly the armor worn by Saul, Israel's tallest man! He took it all off and put on the clothing he was used to—that of a shepherd protecting his sheep.

David wore a sling, a shepherd's stick, and a bag over his shoulder. A sling may not appear to be much, yet it was a powerful weapon. It was a perfect weapon for a shepherd, consisting of a little pouch at the end of two long leather straps. He'd put a stone in the pouch, spin it around his head at breakneck speed, and then let go of one of the straps, tossing the stone with deadly precision. This weapon was so effective that armies would employ slinger divisions.

David went to meet his attacker, now fully outfitted. As he stooped in the dry riverbed on the valley bottom and picked five little, smooth stones, we can only picture David's intense prayers. Then he dashed onto the battleground, not walking but running!

What did Goliath think when he saw his foe? "Because he was only a ruddy and lovely boy," we read, "he scowled at him in contempt." "Am I a dog that you're coming at me with sticks?" Goliath exclaimed. He noticed David's staff but didn't notice the sling. In the name of the Philistine gods, he cursed David and promised to feed the corpse of this despicable opponent to the birds and beasts of the field.

David's response remains a powerful expression of faith to this day. Consider what the small boy would say to Goliath: You're coming at me with swords, spears, and javelins, but I'm coming at you in the name of Jehovah of armies, the God of Israel's battle line, whom you've mocked." David understood that human strength and armament were insignificant. Goliath had disobeyed God, and God would retaliate. "The fight belongs to God," David said.

David was aware of Goliath's size and weapons. Despite this, David refused to be intimidated. He didn't make the same mistakes that Saul and his soldiers did. David did not make the comparison to Goliath. Instead, he considered Goliath in light of God. Goliath towered over other men, standing nine and a half feet (2.9 m) tall, but how huge was he in comparison to the Sovereign of the universe? He was barely more than an insect, like any other human—in this case, one that God was about to destroy! David dashed at his opponent, grabbing a stone from his bag. He slung his sling over his head and twisted it around until it whistled. Goliath advanced toward David, possibly followed by his shield-bearer. Goliath's tremendous height may have been a disadvantage to him since a normal-sized shield-bearer would have struggled to raise a shield high enough to cover the giant's head. And that is precisely what David intended. David let go of his stone. Imagine the silence as it approached its target. God most likely made sure David didn't have to throw another one. Goliath's forehead was struck by the stone, which sank into it. The colossus fell facedown to the ground! The shield-bearer was most likely terrified and ran. David arrived, grabbed Goliath's sword, and used it to sever the giant's skull.

Saul and his warriors finally found their courage. They charged the Philistines with a great battle cry. The fight played out just as David had predicted: "God... will deliver all of you into our hand."

JONATHAN: MORE THAN A BROTHER

The Bible has accounts of imperfect people who demonstrated genuine kindness. Take Jonathan and David as an example. "Jonathan and David grew bonded together in close friendship, and Jonathan began to love him as himself." (1 Samuel 18:1) David was chosen to succeed King Saul. After that, Saul grew enraged with David and attempted to murder him. Jonathan, Saul's son, did not participate in his father's murderous campaign against David. When he finished speaking to Saul, Jonathan's spirit was connected to David's soul, and Jonathan loved him as himself.

That day, Saul took him and refused to allow him to return to his father's house. Jonathan then formed a vow with David because he adored him. Jonathan pulled off his robe and handed it over to David, along with his armor, which included his sword and bow, and his belt. So, David flourished wherever Saul sent him, and Saul appointed him as commander of the army. Jonathan and David agreed to stay friends and support one another.

When we examine some of the reasons that may have stopped Jonathan and David from being friends, their heartfelt attachment is all the more astounding. Jonathan, for example, was 30 years older than David. Jonathan may have concluded that he and this considerably younger and less experienced man had nothing in common. Jonathan, on the other hand, did not regard or consider David as a lesser.

Jonathan could have been envious of David. Jonathan may have claimed that he was the rightful heir to the throne as King Saul's son. Jonathan, on the other hand, was humble and devoted to Jehovah. As a result, he wholeheartedly backed God's choice of David as the future king. He was likewise faithful to David, even though this infuriated Saul. Jonathan had a special fondness for David and did not regard him as a rival. Jonathan admired David for his strength and confidence in God, rather than being envious of him. Jonathan has put his life on the line and faced his father's wrath on numerous occasions to defend his friend. Jonathan was a brave warrior and a superb archer. He and his father, Saul, were known for being "faster than eagles" and "mightier than lions." As a result, Jonathan could have boasted about his valiant deeds. Jonathan was neither competitive nor resentful. Jonathan, on the other hand, appreciated David's bravery and faith in God. After David slew Goliath, he began to adore David as himself

Saul Begins To Loathe David.

Following that, Saul appointed David as commander of the army. David was finally honored more than the king himself in song. As a result, Saul developed distrust and envious loathing toward David. Saul 'began behaving like a prophet' one time while David was playing the harp. Not that Saul began to prophesy, but he displayed unusual feelings and a physical disturbance similar to that of a prophet shortly before or while prophesying. Saul twice hurled a spear at David while in that strange, disturbing mood. After failing to pin David to the wall, Saul eventually agreed to give his daughter Michal in marriage to David in exchange for a hundred Philistine foreskins. When Saul made this offer, he intended for David to perish at their hands. The plan failed when David presented not 100, but 200 foreskins to make a marital partnership with Saul. David was a successful leader, and Saul's jealousy grew as his reputation grew. In the hopes that the Philistines will murder David, Saul gives David his daughter Michal in marriage if David kills one hundred Philistines. After the wedding, Saul sends assassins to the newlyweds' quarters, but David manages to flee with Michal's help. Despite a handful of brief reconciliations, David remains an exile and an outlaw. King's terror and loathing for him have grown. Saul expressed his desire to kill David to his son Jonathan and all of his servants. Saul promised not to kill David after Jonathan intervened. Despite this, David was forced to escape for his life when Saul flung his third spear at him. Saul even had messengers keep an eye on David's house and ordered that he be killed the next morning. When David's allies realized that Saul had declared war on him, they utilized military strategy to protect him. Michal, Saul's daughter, assisted her husband David in escaping via a window. "He is unwell," she announced as she held back Saul's officers. With Achish the king of Gath, David sought protection in Philistia. David got scared of wolves after the Philistines realized who he was and indicated to the king that he was a security concern. "So, he pretended to be insane in their presence and began acting insane in their hands, putting cross marks on the gate doors and letting his saliva drip down his beard." King Achish declined to have him in his presence and allowed him to go about his business as a harmless idiot. 21:13 -1 Samuel 21:13

Saul's Life Is Saved By David.

The people of Ziph reported to Saul at Gibeah that David was hiding in the Hachilah Hills, which are east of Jeshimon. Saul then went for David with three thousand soldiers. Saul and his troops camped in the Ziph wilderness. When David learned that Saul was pursuing him, he dispatched spies into the wilderness to confirm his location, and the report he received was affirmative. That night, David and Abishai entered Saul's camp and saw him sleeping, for the Lord had placed a deep sleep over him and his army. Saul's spear was lodged by his head on the ground, while his commander, Abner, and his troops were sleeping around him. Abishai saw this as an opportunity to get rid of Saul by claiming that God had given him to David. He asked David for permission to pin Saul down with a single strike and kill him, but David refused. Instead, David said that Saul should be permitted to live since he was the Lord's anointed and hence should not be harmed. According to David, God would murder him at the appropriate time, or he would die in combat, or he would die a natural death when his life came to an end. As a result, they permitted Saul to live. They did, however, take Saul's spear and water jar. David moved to the other side of the hill, separating himself from Saul's camp. Then he chastised Abner for putting the king in danger by failing to protect him. He explained how someone had broken into the camp without their knowledge. Abner was asked by David to check for the king's spear and water jar.

When Saul heard David's voice, he felt terrible. He addressed him by name. David inquired as to why Saul had been pursuing him. If the Lord sent him, he should accept a sacrifice and let it go, but if men stirred his soul to pursue him, the Lord must curse those men. Saul became penitent. He was sorry for all he had done, including chasing David down to kill him. He promised not to pursue him again and invited him to return because he, David, had placed Saul's life in his hands as a valuable asset. David requested that Abner dispatch one of his men to collect the king's spear and water container. Saul wished David well and predicted that he would succeed in life.

This is the prudent and correct path to adopt. David demonstrated this in his relationship with King Saul, who pursued him and attempted to kill him several times. As it were, David could have taken the law into his own hands. He had the chance to kill King Saul on two occasions, but he chose not to. Saul's persecution of David is without a doubt a burden to him.

CHAPTER THREE
DAVID'S VICTORIES
Fear

The two men had parted ways after Saul promised not to harm David again. David continued on his way, while Saul returned to his position. David had been delivered from Saul several times by God. David's anointing as the king should have provided him the certainty that God would protect him. David was terrified because he had lost faith in Saul and his promise. His faith in God for his safety was shaken by his terror. "I shall now fall one day by the hand of Saul," David declared, it appears that he was no longer relying on God for assistance. David knew he couldn't keep running from Saul in his current strength.

Is this the same David who declared, "Jehovah is my strength; whom shall I fear?" (Psalm 27:1) "Some rely upon chariots, and some in horses," David said, "but we shall remember the name of our God" (Psalm:20:7)? Didn't David once remark, "Whatever time I am terrified, I shall trust in you" (Psalm 56:3)? David had become discouraged at this point. He decided to flee to Philistia, away from Saul and his army.

The Philistines' Homeland

Going into the country of the Philistines was a difficult task for David. Their king, Achish of Gath, was also someone David feared ([1 Samuel:21:12]; [Psalms:56:1-13]). David's despondency drove him to flee his ancient homeland and the fellowship of the other Children of Israel. David and his 600 warriors and their families stayed in Philistine territory for a year and four months. David lived in Ziklag, which was given to him by Achish, king of Gath.

A Servant

People throughout the world enjoy having one of God's followers alongside them. They are confident that God will protect His people. Because of just one believer among them, they hope to obtain God's favor. David and his troops appeared to be treated well by Achish, who allowed them to settle in his country and gave them the city of Ziklag. Achish did so because he expected to benefit from David's presence in his territory. Achish was not concerned with David's welfare. David was a brave warrior and a capable soldier. Achish realized that by fighting their enemies, David might do a lot of good for the Philistines. David had fled to the country of the Philistines to avoid Saul, but he was forced to fight for the Philistines and risk his life. By being so dejected as to reside among the Philistines, David gained nothing. "He has made his people Israel despise him." (I Samuel: 27:12).

In Danger

The Philistines were at war with the Children of Israel at the time. David was appointed as Achish's bodyguard and guardian of the king's head ([1 Samuel: 28:2]). David found himself in a tight spot as a result of his connection with ungodly people. How many times have individuals who abandon God's people found themselves in serious trouble? Children occasionally get themselves into problems because they choose wicked friends. "Enter not into the road of the wicked, and go not in the way of evil men,"

Solomon warns (Proverbs 4:14), and "Do not envy the evil persons, nor seek to be with them" (Proverbs:24:1).

David may have argued with himself over what he should do. Should he decline to fight the Children of Israel in battle? Should he stay at home, ungrateful for all Achish had done for him, like a coward? Is David a traitor to his people, or not? Should he fight Israel as an adversary? Isn't that what makes David unfit to rule? Would David be held responsible if Saul was killed? Perhaps, when David contemplated the situation, it appeared that anything he did would be riddled with sin and scandal. Was there a way out for David that didn't involve guilt or grief?

The King's Defense

David and his troops were assigned to serve as Achish's rearguard. David was most likely just meant to serve as the king's bodyguard. It's unlikely that David intended to participate in any other way in the Philistine-Israeli fight. Among the Philistines, David had led a blameless and upright life. He was in an unusual situation. Without a question, he looked to God for guidance in doing the right thing.

The Philistine princes stood against David and his men. They demanded that David be excused from fighting with them. The Philistines were terrified that once David and his soldiers were in the baths, they would turn on them. They had been opponents in the past, and they believed David was more dangerous than Saul. Perhaps they remembered David as the one who had defeated Goliath, their champion. Achish released David and his warriors to please the Philistine princes. Achish had a positive impression of David's life. Achish had not discovered any flaws or bad in him. David's behavior and the association had delighted and gratified Achish. Achish ordered David and his soldiers to leave early in the morning so as not to enrage the Philistines. So God delivered David from the Philistine army and the conflict between the Philistines and Israel.

Their Home

David and his soldiers hurried to Ziklag, their hometown. They marched for three days. They were most likely fatigued and wanted to get home. What a depressing sight they saw! The Amalekites had besieged Ziklag, captured all of the residents, and set fire to the city while they were gone. David and his troops, these great and brave warriors, were overcome with grief and wept. David and his men cared deeply for their children and their homes. It's no surprise that the men sobbed because their families had been taken away and their homes had been destroyed.

Correction

Perhaps God allowed the devastation of Ziklag and the enslavement of the people to teach David a lesson. There is no evidence that David prayed or inquired of God about his decision to live among the Philistines. David appeared to have doubts about God's ability to protect him from Saul. God did not allow David or his family to be killed while among the Philistines, although they did suffer. "For whom God loves disciplines." ([Hebrews: 12:6]).

Today, God deems it necessary to allow hardship and pain for the sake of His people. This does not imply that God has turned away from us. It's God's method of bringing us closer to Himself. God loves us and wants us to grow in our faith in Him. God loves us and wants us to grow in our faith in Him.

David's family has never been molested while he was gone on duty previously, as far as we knew. David's family has been cared for and safeguarded by God. David was not in the way of duty this time. Being away from home was his idea. God had not ordered him to leave, and duty had not demanded his absence.

God's Encouragement

The Bible says that David encouraged himself in this God. When everything seemed to be working against David, he turned to God.

Saul had expelled David from his homeland. David had been sacked from the Philistine army. The Amalekites had pillaged his city and captured David's family. David's friends then turned against him, threatening to stone him. David knew what to do in such a difficult situation. He believed in God. Perhaps David had learned a lesson since he prayed this time. David enquired about God and demonstrated that he was relying on God for assistance. "Shall I pursue after these soldiers?" David questioned God specifically. "Pursue," God told David, "Because you shall certainly overtake them, and without fail reclaim all." Some people may not receive specific responses to their prayers because they pray in a generic manner rather than a specific prayer. David got a clear word and promise from God.

Amalekites' Pursuit

David's faith and patience were appreciated by the 600 disgruntled men who were with him. He treated them well, so they followed him while he chased the Amalekites. Some of these men were so exhausted that they couldn't keep up with David as he tried to catch up to those who had taken away his family and belongings. David did not encourage his men to exceed their limits. One-third of David's troops remained behind at the Besor brook.

Mercy And Assistance

David treated a young Egyptian he found in a field with kindness. David showed mercy by feeding and watering him. Some individuals would have been in a haste to aid the young man and would have dismissed his problems as unimportant. Because David took his time and made provisions for the young man, he was rewarded with information. The Egyptian had been an Amalekite's servant and had taught David everything he needed to know. When the Egyptian fell ill, his master abandoned him. The young man was now capable and willing to help people who had befriended him as well as punish his master, who had abused him.

Nothing Was Lost.

The Egyptian man led David to the Amalekites' camp, where they were celebrating their loot from David's city. When the Amalekites thought they were safe and had forgotten about war, David surprised them and caught them off guard when they were unable to make much of a fight. Only 400 of them made it out alive, while David recaptured what the Amalekites had taken.

The riches were retrieved, and the family was rescued. David gained a lot of spoils while losing nothing. He Trusted in God

May we be reminded of how much better David did when he prayed and trusted God. When David went to the Philistines' territory, he became a servant and was forced to fight. When David put his trust in God, all of his enemies' plans fell apart. No weapon designed against David could flourish as long as he believed in God ([Isaiah: 54:17]). The same will happen in our lives when we are willing to trust and rely on God.

Sharing The Spoil

Those who had remained by the brook Besor greeted David and his warriors as they returned. Though they were unable to accompany David, they were pleased with the work that had been accomplished.

However, there were some bad individuals with David who were selfish and greedy. They were willing to reunite the families with those who had stayed, but not with the spoils. David disregarded his men's advice. He assured them that they would all share the prizes out of thankfulness to God, who had assisted and protected them. It would only be fair and just to distribute the rewards among those who stayed with the "things." On that day, David enacted an ordinance and law stating that everyone would receive an equal part of the award and spoils.

CHAPTER FOUR
SAUL TAKES HIS OWN LIFE.

The Bible devotes many chapters to King Saul's life and death so that everyone who reads it understands how dreadful it is to be a backslider and a rebel against God.

Saul had a lot going for him in terms of natural beauty and his attractive physique. There were numerous reasons to believe that Saul's life could have been of tremendous benefit and value to God's cause, yet it did not. Saul got exalted in the high position of the king that God had bestowed upon him, and despite God's best efforts to correct, lead, and maintain him in his difficulties, Saul became a dreadful failure. Because of Saul's repeated disobedience to God's Word, God took the kingdom of Israel from him and gave it to David. Instead of repenting of his transgressions that were causing him so much trouble, Saul let his sons drive him to a lost eternity of suicide. "When the evil spirit is gone out of a man, he walks through parched places, seeking rest; and finding none, he says, I will return unto my house where I came out," Jesus once said. "When he arrives, it has been swept and garnished. Then he takes seven other spirits who are more wicked than himself, and they come and stay there, and that man's last state is worse than his first " (Luke:11:24-26).

Saul had been truly converted; God had renewed his heart, and he prophesied when the Spirit of the Lord came upon him (1 Samuel 10: 9, 10). Despite this, Saul's heart was filled with wickedness, and when he refused to repent of his wrongdoings, he became a willing tool of the devil "For whom a man is overpowered, he is brought into servitude" (2 Peter:2:19). Saul became a bad man as a backslider and a rebel against God's government. His good deeds became rare rather than becoming a habit of daily existence, and his stubborn pride drove him to ever-worse deeds. He got arrogant in his wrongdoing, and his misdeeds grew out of private envy of David until he was pursuing David openly, with the stated purpose of killing him as soon as possible. During one of Saul's reigns, he became enraged and bloodthirsty because David had eluded him with the help of Ahimelech the priest. Saul slaughtered Ahimelech and his household, as well as many priests and inhabitants of Nob, and the city was set on fire. Because of his evil heart, Saul did all these things. (1 Samuel: 22:18, 19). Saul's cruelty was without mercy. God promises, "Vengeance is mine; I will repay," and Saul's rebellion, his ruthless pursuit of David, his uncontrollable rage that drove him to attempt to kill his son, and the real murder of God's priests did not go ignored or unpunished by God.

The End Of Kingdom

Saul was killed in instant combat between the Philistines and the Israelites. God's judgment was carried out through the Philistines, who were selected by God to carry out His Word against Saul.

Saul had been mortally wounded by Philistine archers, and to prevent falling into their hands, he asked his armor-bearer to murder him. This he refused to do, so Saul stabbed himself with his armor bearer's sword and died. His armor-bearer followed suit, and they both died by their own hands. Doeg, the Edomite, who slaughtered the priests at Nob, is said to have been Saul's amour bearer, according to tradition. If that was the case, divine justice was served to them both when they perished with the same sword that they used to kill the priests of God.

Philistine Victory

Saul despised God's way and died a shameful death as a result. His opponents heaped blame and dishonor upon him. The Philistines took his body and the bodies of his sons and transported them away to Beth Shan, where they were chained to a wall so that everyone could view them. It was a huge win for the Philistines, and one of Israel's most humiliating defeats to that point. The cup of God's anger was poured out on Saul, and he drank until the last bitter dregs.

Heroic Acts

Saul committed a few good things in his life, and one of them resulted in a return, even though he was dead. The Ammonites had previously invaded the city of Jabesh Gilead, and only Saul's prompt intervention spared their lives and their houses ([1 Samuel: 11:1-11]). Hearing of the horrible treatment of Saul and his sons' bodies by the Philistines, these men went to the enemy's city in the dead of night and collected their bodies. As a result of a previous act of compassion, Saul was given a dignified burial.

David's Discontent

David's godly patience and forgiveness while being persecuted by Saul is a magnificent example of the true spirit of the Gospel of Jesus Christ, and David was saddened to learn of Saul's untimely death. David's grief was genuine and unfeigned, and he was especially heartbroken over Jonathan, one of Saul's sons. Jonathan and David were good friends, and David was devastated to learn of his friend's death. God does not delight in the death of the wicked, and neither do God's people delight in the notion of a soul being lost for all eternity. Some argue that David would have been right if he rejoiced that his adversary was dead, allowing him to take control of the kingdom without further struggle. However, vengeance has never been a component of the Gospel of Jesus Christ.

David waited for the Lord to deliver him from Saul's insane hatred, and God did so without David having to strike back. The tremendous difference between David's frame of mind and that of the Amalekite which made him inform David that he was the one who had killed Saul may be observed in David's response to such a revelation. The Amalekite expected to be rewarded for being the executioner of the rejected Saul as well as the bearer of such news to David; but he was dealing with a man of God, not a man filled with evil, revenge, and violence. The fact that these men had perished and, except Jonathan, had been pushed into a lost eternity was not pleasant news to David. A Christian would rather suffer a great deal at the hands of evil persons than be the cause of someone being cut off prematurely in his sins.

Anointed By God

Instead of gaining favor with David, the Amalekite lost his own life when he told

David he was the one who had killed Saul. "How were you not scared to extend your hand to harm God's anointed?" David inquired. He then ordered one of his men to attack him and kill him. "His blood will be on your head," David warned him, "for your mouth has testified against you, saying, I have slain God's anointed." As a result of his deception, the Amalekite died.

The Bow's Song

David's anguish over the death of his companion Jonathan and the untimely death of Saul is expressed in a lamentation. This is commonly referred to as the "Song of the Bow." Because of their victory against Israel and the murder of Saul, David believed the Philistines would be overjoyed. It had been a horrible day for Israel. Israel had requested and received a king, but he had become a nightmare to them rather than a blessing. Israel has been punished by God for rejecting Him. Saul's resistance and sin brought him to the hour of judgment. Saul had provided abundant opportunity for the pagan nations to throw shame upon the name of Jehovah, Israel's God. This clarifies David's song: "Tell it not in Gath, broadcast it not in the streets of Ashkelon; lest the Philistines' girls celebrate, lest the daughters of the uncircumcised triumph." But, despite David's precautions, Saul's body was hanging in disgrace and disrepute in the streets of Beth Shan at the time.

David Crowned The King Of All Israel.

Mourning For Saul And Jonathan

David was heartbroken about the deaths of Saul and Jonathan. He paid homage to his former king and rival, Saul, and was saddened by the death of Saul's son, Jonathan. David expressed his sorrow by penning a song about their tremendous acts. He called Jonathan "my brother Jonathan" and recalled Jonathan's generosity and love for him. David would become king as a result of Saul's death, as he had already been anointed by God. Even though Saul's death meant victory for David, he showed no joy or pleasure that his foe was dead. When David's adversary fell, he did not celebrate (Proverbs 24:17).

Prayer

David may have dispatched messengers across Israel, requesting that the people swear allegiance to him as king. David did not act in this manner. He awaited the fulfillment of God's promise. In both times of blessing and hardship, David prayed and inquired of God. While waiting for God, David did not sit back and do nothing; instead, he did everything that was asked of him. David asked God if he should visit any of Judah's cities.   God commanded David to leave. David did not visit his hometown, Bethlehem, or any other location he could have preferred. God led David to Hebron, the city of the Priests and a place of refuge.

In Peace And War.

David took the men who had joined him in exile with him   Those who were in debt and dissatisfied had appointed David as their captain (I Samuel 22:2). These people had stood with David in his moments of need and hiding. When David became king, he remembered those who had helped him along the way. They had been afflicted because of David and had shared his hunger and misery. This devoted band would now reign alongside him. The Bible says that those who are faithful and obedient to Christ, as well as those who suffer for the sake of Him, shall reign with Him. (2 Timothy 2:12).

King Of Judah

David was anointed king by the house of Judah, and his people, after he, his men, and their families had moved to Hebron. David was anointed asking for the second time. He had been anointed by Samuel some ten years ago, at God's command. The anointing was done by the people of Judah, who were members of Israel's children. David ruled over the house of Judah at Hebron for seven and a half years. David made friends with the men of Jabesh-Gilead during this period and praised them for their kindness to their former king, Saul, whom they had buried.

David expressed God's favor and goodwill to them. He modestly informed them that he had succeeded Saul as king.

Sons Of Saul

As was customary, David did not dispose of all of Saul's relatives. In those days, it was considered necessary to kill the descendants of the previous king to establish one's kingdom. David did not harm any of Saul's family members. In that regard, there was no ruler like David. Some of Saul's sons were killed in combat, while others were killed later, but none were killed by David in any scheme. Representatives from Israel's tribes assembled in Hebron. They were united in their desire to make David king (I Chronicles

12:38). David was God's choice as well as the people's decision. They stayed at Hebron for three days to ally with David, begging him to be their ruler. They presented three reasons for wanting David to be both their king and the king of Judah. They were related as Children of Israel. It was God's law that their king is one of their own, not a foreigner (Deuteronomy 17:15). "We are your bone and your flesh," they reminded David, qualifying him to be their king.

Another reason was that they were reminded of David's previous good service to the Children of Israel. He had been diligent in doing whatever he could for the Children of Israel. Perhaps they were referring to David's killing of Goliath, when the entire army, including the king, was terrified of the hostile giant.

The Israelites gave the third most essential argument. God anointed David and appointed him. In both peace and battle, he was to reign. "You shall feed my people Israel, and you shall be a leader over Israel," the Lord promised David.

King Over Our Lives

It was in everyone's hearts to make David king over them. Nobody could think of a reason why David shouldn't be king. In today's world, there is One who would reign supreme. There is no reason why we should not make Jesus the King of our lives. Some make justifications, but none of them are acceptable. There are numerous reasons why Jesus should rule in our hearts and lives, arguments that are similar to those offered by those who chose David to be their king. Those who accept Jesus as their King is called brothers. The only one who can liberate us from the enemy and remove sin from our lives is Jesus. "Behold the Lamb of God, who takes away the sin of the world," John the Baptist declared, looking at Jesus (John 1:29). As a shepherd tends to his flock, Jesus leads and nourishes His people with the bread of life. "I am the bread of life: he who comes to me shall never want, and he who believes in me shall never thirst" (John 6:35). God's plan for our salvation is Jesus. God gave him, anointed him, and honored him. Jesus will ascend to the throne as King of kings and Lord of lords (I Timothy 6:15). Why not make Jesus the ruler and king of your heart and life right now?

Reign Of David

The covenant made by David and all the elders of Israel was witnessed by God. David was anointed as a king for the third time. David began his rule when he was thirty years old. He was the same age as the Levites when they were called to work in the Tabernacle for God (Numbers 4:47). When Jesus began His public ministry, he was the same age as David (Luke 3:23). David ruled for four decades. Hebron, a prominent city throughout the history of the Children of Israel, was where he spent part of his reign. It had witnessed several memorable moments. Abraham constructed an altar to God in Hebron. Sarah, his wife, died there and was buried in the family tomb in the nearby cave of Machpelah (Genesis 12:8; 23:2,19, 20). Caleb inherited Hebron because he completely followed God. (Joshua I4: 14). Hebron was thereafter handed to the Levites and it became a city of refuge (Joshua 21:11-13).

In Jerusalem, David ruled for a longer time. It became the capital and is even more well-known than Hebron, having been referenced in the Bible near the conclusion. It was almost in the heart of the Holy Land. "Beautiful for situation, the pleasure of the whole earth is mount Zion," the Psalmist wrote about Jerusalem (Psalm 48:2). Jerusalem was located on a high tableland, about twenty Roman miles north of Hebron, and was a mountain city through which all travelers passing through Palestine passed. Because the Lord's Temple was erected there, Jerusalem was regarded as a holy place of worship. God listened and answered prayers offered in that location and for that city (2Chronicles 7:12-15).

The Ark Of The Covenant

The chosen men of Israel met once more with David, their king. They all agreed that moving the Ark of the Lord was the correct and good thing to do (I Chronicles 13:3, 4). The Ark had been abandoned by the Children of Israel for many years in Abinadab's house. The Ark was a sign of God's presence, and it had been a gift to them when it was in their midst. When the Philistines got their hands on the Ark, they were in a lot of trouble. What may be a benefit to God's people may be a curse to the rest of the world! God's Word gives us life and gives death to those who do not obey it. David had excellent intentions when he brought the Ark to Jerusalem, but there is no indication of him asking God for guidance in removing this holy sign of God's presence. The Children of Israel were noble in their desire for God's presence in their midst. The presence of God leads to forgiveness of sin and salvation. God's presence offers calm, assurance, protection, and hope. There is nothing except emptiness without God.

The Wrong Approach

The desire for the Ark of God to be with David and the Children of Israel was not a mistake. Doing God's work in God's manner was the lesson they needed to learn. They set the Ark on a new wagon driven by Abinadab's sons Uzzah and Ahio. According to the Law, it was supposed to be carried on the Levites' shoulders. It was transported by the Children of Israel in the same way that it had been moved by the Philistines (I Samuel 6:7, 8). How many people have suffered because they followed the example of those around them rather than obeying God's command?

God Has Struck Me.

The Children of Israel were overjoyed as they carried the Ark closer to Jerusalem. They sang praises to God, and the musicians gave their best. They were suddenly filled with terror and grief. The oxen tripped, and the Ark rattled on the wagon. Uzzah reached out to hold the Ark -- and then died. God had said that those who carried the Ark should "not touch any holy thing, lest they perish" (Numbers 4:15). Uzzah came close to touching the Ark and was struck by God, dying beside it. Uzzah may have had good intentions in trying to keep the Ark steady, but he was abandoning his right to be present at the Ark. There would have been no need for Uzzah to touch it if it had been carried according to God's instructions. Uzzah's mistake demonstrated that good intentions do not always justify poor behavior.

God's Method

David was both perplexed and terrified. The Ark was kept at the house of Obed Edom, the Gittite, lest God strikes them all down. The Lord's blessing came with the Ark. Obed Edom and his household discovered that serving God pays off, as they were blessed while in possession of the Ark. David appealed to God and inquired about moving the Ark. Uzzah would not have died at this time if he had prayed the first time, and they would have received God's blessing sooner. David built a tent for the Ark and prepared a space for it. The Children of Israel brought the Ark to Jerusalem after three months. This time they carried it on the shoulders of the Levites (Numbers 7:9; I Chronicles 15:2, 12-

15), covered in badgers' skins (Numbers 4:6), and borne on staves, as God had instructed (Exodus 25:14). The Ark was put in the tabernacle that had been built for it, and sacrifices of praise and thankfulness were made to God. The Children of Israel were successful when the Ark was moved in a way that delighted God. Because they were obedient, there was a lot of joy.

CHAPTER FIVE

DAVID COMMITS ADULTERY WITH BATH-SHEBA

David and Bathsheba's story reminds us that even great men who have been called by God are still human and battle with sin. The story begins with King David choosing to remain in Jerusalem while the rest of the Israelite army is sent to fight other nations and kingdoms. When David is sitting on the palace roof, he notices a lovely woman bathing on her roof. David was immediately drawn to her and dispatched messengers to ascertain her identity. The messengers returned and informed David that she was Bathsheba, Eliam's daughter, and Uriah's wife. Though David was aware of her marital status, he sent for her and slept with her. Bathsheba subsequently informs David that she is expecting a child.

Uriah Is Sent To His Death.

David was worried that his adultery would now be exposed. Uriah was summoned by the King to return home and spend the night with his wife, Bathsheba, to cover up the fact that Bathsheba was pregnant with David's child. Uriah, on the other hand, refused to sleep with his wife while his fellow soldiers were fighting. David was furious that his strategy had failed. When Uriah returned to battle, King David sent a message to the army commander, instructing him to place Uriah on the front lines and retreat so that he would die. Bathsheba was brought to King David to be his wife after her husband's death. God sent the prophet Nathan to confront David when the child of David and

Bathsheba was born. Nathan told a parable about a rich man who killed a poor man's only sheep despite having many flocks of his own. David agreed that the man that committed such an act deserves to die. David was visibly enraged because he was formerly a shepherd and he believe the story is real. "Because he committed such a thing and showed no mercy, he must pay for that lamb four times over" (2 Samuel 12:5,6). Nathan then pointed to David and said, "You are the one!" (See 2 Samuel 12:7) David was the one who had committed this transgression, and his house would suffer the consequences in the form of continual violence. "Jehovah has taken away your sin," Nathan stated after David repented (see Psalm 51). You will not pass away. But because you have demonstrated total disrespect for God by doing this, your son will die." Giving in to sin hardens the heart and causes the Holy Spirit to leave. Taking a man's reason is worse than taking his money, and luring him into sin is worse than luring him into any kind of worldly difficulties.

What Were The Repercussions Of David's Deeds?

There is no denying that, despite being "a man after God's own heart," David abused his power and disobeyed God's rule. David's journey moved from achievement to achievement before his encounter with Bathsheba. He killed beasts, fought Goliath, was hailed as a great warrior by the people and was crowned King of all Israel and Judah. However, his life was filled with pain and betrayal following his crime. The son of David and Bathsheba died. David's son, Amnon, raped his daughter Tamar, who was eventually slain by her brother, Absalom. Absalom betrayed David and staged a brilliant coup d'état to seize the throne. Absalom also raped the concubines of his father David and exiled David. David is finally restored, but he is bitter and has given Solomon orders to wreak vengeance on his adversaries. Even after his death, another son, Adonijah, is killed in the succession conflict.

His Son Betrayed Him
A Handsome Prince

"No one was more beautiful than Absalom in all of Israel: from the sole of his foot to the crown of his head, there was no flaw in him" (2 Samuel 14:25). Men may be swept away by a person's external appearance like Absalom did Israel's heart, but God focuses on the heart" (1 Samuel 16:73). God could see awful pride beneath the grandeur and pomp of this gorgeous prince, who rode his elaborate chariot down the packed street while fifty men cleared the way in front of him. A Judas kiss was hidden underneath the embellished greeting. This office-seeking, the hand-shaking vote-stealing politician said, "Oh, that I was made judge in the land."

Duplicity

This foolish prince traveled to Hebron with a deceptive heart and the guise of paying a vow to God to wrest the throne from his God-chosen and divinely anointed father, David. How easily Israel's citizens were deceived! Oh, the vainness of a flawless exterior when we stand before the Almighty! "I am wealthy and well-endowed, and require nothing," a people formerly described by God as "wretched, miserable, and impoverished, blind, and naked."

David Flees

Absalom won the hearts of Israel's men with flattery and fair words. His crafty intellect must have planned his father's betrayal for years. David appeared unconcerned by his overindulged son's conduct. Absalom and David are such opposites! Absalom declared himself king at Hebron amid the sound of bugles and pomp. "As David went up the Mount Olivet, he was wailing and his head was covered, and he went barefoot: and all the people who were with him covered every man's head, and they went up, weeping as they went up" [2 Samuel:15:30]. David told the priests and Levites carrying the Ark of the covenant, "Carry back the ark of God into the city: if I shall find favor in the eyes of the

God, he will bring me back, and let me see it and its habitation: but if he therefore says, I have no delight in you; behold, here am I, let him do to me as seemed well to him" [2 Samuel:15:25,26]. David appeared to believe that God was punishing him for his previous wrongdoing during the affair. "Behold, I will raise evil against you from your own house," said Nathan the Prophet when delivering God's message to David. David accepted God's chastisement with humility and resignation. How few men are willing to accept rebuke like David!

Shimei's Disgraceful Behavior

Shimei of the family of Saul cursed David and flung stones at his company as if the pain of losing the kingdom and the treachery by his beloved son weren't enough. "So let him curse since the LORD hath said unto him,

Curse David," David restrained the courageous warriors with him who were willing to deal with him. [2 Samuel: 16:10-12]). Isn't it possible that David's humility justifies Peter's words? "For it is praiseworthy if a man endures anguish, suffering unfairly, for the sake of conscience before God." What honor is it if, when you are plagued by your flaws, you patiently accept them? But if you do well and suffer for it patiently, God will accept it". - 1 Peter 2:19; 1 Peter 2:20.

Absalom's Last Days

David arranged his defense into three divisions and put commanders over thousands after a journey of more than sixty miles from Jerusalem, indicating that a large army accompanied him out of Jerusalem. On that day, David's servants killed 20,000 people, but Absalom, the revolt's commander, met with an unusual fate. Absalom died while riding a mule. 2 Samuel 18:9.

David's Sadness

David's profound affection for his rebellious son is shown in his words after hearing of Absalom's death: "O my son Absalom, my son Absalom, my son Absalom!" O Absalom, my son, my son, if only I had died!" 2 Samuel 18:33.

Shimei Asks For Forgiveness

When David's triumphant soldiers returned to Jerusalem, who should meet them first but Shimei, the man who had fiercely abused the king? He knelt in humble repentance before David. Even though Abishai, one of David's generals, rightfully demanded Shimei's life, the king turned to Shimei and replied, "You shall not die."

CHAPTER SIX

DAVID PRAISES GOD

NOTES:

This is a Messianic Psalm, which means it is a Psalm about Christ and informs us anything about Him, His official tasks, or his coming to earth. David was praising God for freeing him from his afflictions and granting him victory over his foes, while also offering us a magnificent prophecy about the Messiah. Many connections exist between David's experiences and Christ's life. David went through a period of humiliation and suffering at the hands of Saul. On this earth, Jesus likewise went through a period of humiliation and suffering. He was carried to the slaughter "like a lamb," but He rose victorious over death, destruction, and the grave. David did not follow Jesus' example throughout his life, but in his dealings with Saul, David was blameless and showed much charity to Saul.

A Refuge And A Rock

David presented his testimony at the start of this song. He wrote about his relationship with God. "God is my refuge and my stronghold," he revealed his thoughts. When David was fleeing Saul and crawling across those jagged rocks, he recognized how much of a stronghold they were to him. To his soul, God was just such a stronghold. When the enemy of his soul arrived on one side, David was often practically surrounded and almost taken, but when God led him to the other side, he was able to escape. As a result, God was always his refuge.

Horn Of Salvation

"God is my armor and the horn of my salvation." In the Bible, a horn represents power. It is an ox's natural, God-given weapon, as well as its defense and might. Many other animals have this trait. As a result, the heads of governments are frequently referred to in Scripture as horns. "The horn of my salvation" refers to salvation that possesses both forceful and efficient features. This magnificent salvation that God has provided for us has no flaws. We are set free from the power and rule of sin because of it. It takes a powerful deliverer to free any soul from Satan's traps and the basic and wicked habits that sin has enslaved them to. However, the salvation that Jesus Christ has purchased for us is sufficient. It's complete. It has all we require for our ultimate exaltation.

The Waves Of Death

David may have spent many sleepless nights on the mountaintop, in dens, or in caverns while fleeing from Saul. He had to be wondering if he'd ever see the light of day again. David is mentioned in the Epistle to the Hebrews as one of the prophets who "wandered about in sheep-skins and goatskins; being impoverished, afflicted, tormented; in deserts, and mountains, and dens and caves of the ground." The army of Saul or the Philistines, pouring forward like the waves of the sea, may certainly intimidate David. God, however, heard his cries and freed him from all of his fears and dangers.

The Elements Are Furious

The depiction David gives here of how God responded to his prayers for rescue considerably enhances the historical record. These descriptions, however, are not just a record of his conquests, but also a Messianic prophecy, referring to the Savior's death and resurrection. God is described as a warrior who descended from Heaven on the back of a cherub who was carried along by the wind and driven by the tempest. The heavy clouds that covered Him served as His shelter. Thunderbolts, lightning, scorching hail, deluging rains, and wild winds were his weapons. God's fury was depicted by the smoke that came out of His nostrils and the fire that came out of His lips. The earth shuddered and shook. The foundations of the hills were shaken, and the rocks were ripped apart, allowing water to flow freely. Men flee from God's presence when He speaks in this manner. How eerily identical to the events surrounding Jesus' death and resurrection! "There was a tremendous earthquake," the Gospel writer says of these earth-shaking events, "because the angel of God descended from heaven, and came and rolled back the stone from the door, and sat upon it." "For fear of him, the keepers shook, and became as dead men" [Matthew:28:2-4]); and "from the sixth hour, there was darkness over all the land until the ninth hour... And behold, the temple veil was ripped in two from top to bottom; and the ground trembled, and the rocks were split; After his resurrection, the tombs were opened, and many bodies of the saints who had been sleeping awoke and came out of them" [Matthew:27:45]; [Matthew:27:51]-53). What a striking resemblance this language has to the terminology used to describe Christ's advent in His revelation! (Refer to [Revelation 19:11-16.]). We recall that an earthquake opened the jail doors for Paul and Silas at midnight. God will deliver every one of us, just as he did David, Paul, Silas, and countless other holy men and friends of God. His power is unchanged today. His mercy extends to everyone. However, the world has yet to see his true grandeur.

The Reward Of Righteousness

"According to my righteousness, God repaid me." David always dealt with Saul fairly. David never raised his hand against Saul in an attempt to harm him. David would not allow any of his soldiers to hurt Saul at any time. When David was in difficulties, it was his uprightness of heart that gave him confidence. When a person honors his vows to God and stands before Him with clean hands and a pure heart, he can come to God in faith and claim the divine promises in times of hardship. There will be no obstructed faith pathways for him to clear. He will be able to communicate freely with Heaven. When Isaiah advised King Hezekiah that he needed to clean up his residence since he was about to die, he could confidently pray to God to lengthen his days. Hezekiah prayed to God, assuring Him that he had walked before Him in honesty and with a perfect heart and that he had done what was right in His eyes. How fast he got a response from Heaven! When God commanded Isaiah to go tell Hezekiah that He had heard his prayer, he had not yet left the house. Psalms 11:7 says, "The righteous God loves righteousness."

 When trouble occurs, on the other hand, if a man walks carelessly, fails to pay his vows, ceases to renew his consecration, regards iniquity in his heart, or acts evil of any type, he must repeat those vows and consecrations and clear the faith channels of obstructions before he may have faith in God. A good life is a powerful and efficient barricade against the enemies of the soul. (See John 3:18-22.)

Mercy And Gentleness

David wrote about mercy and the responsibility of mercy. At various times, David showed mercy to Saul. "Blessed are the merciful, for they shall gain mercy," the Beatitudes remarked. God honors and rewards those who are merciful in their dealings with others. As we forgive those who trespass against us, God forgives us our sins. Throughout David's troubled days, God taught him to bear and forbear, to act courageously in adversity, and to remain humble even in success. David possessed courage and power as human attributes. But he also enjoyed extraordinary prosperity from God's hand, and no enemy could defeat him while he walked with Him. God was the source of David's deliverances and all of his spiritual and temporal triumphs.

The main theme of this lovely song is expressing thanks to God for conquests and successes. "Great deliverance grants him to his king," Psalms 18:50 says, "and shows mercy to his anointed, David, and his seed forevermore." The genuine King, David, the anointed one, and we, the spiritual seed, are all mentioned here. How vast, high, all-encompassing, and far-reaching is our God's mercy and love!

David was a monarch appointed by God. He was a fighter. But he understood it was because of his God's help that he could "race through a regiment" and leap over a wall. Nonetheless, he understood – as must we – that there are no victories without a war, and no crown without a sacrifice. If we are to inherit eternal life, we must likewise "fight a good fight," as he did.

LAST MOMENTS OF DAVID

Through the prophet Nathan, God made a covenant with David as king. (2 Samuel 7:8-16). David's throne would be eternal. This signifies that a descendant of David would reign over Israel and Judea in perpetuity. If David's descendants sinned, they would face severe punishment. The Messianic Agreement is the interpretation of this covenant. We know that Jesus was descended from David's lineage. David was delighted that he had received such a wonderful promise from God. David lived in a magnificent palace and lamented the fact that God lacked a suitable temple. A tent was used to house the Ark of the Covenant. David began drafting designs for God's temple. David chose the temple's location and gathered construction supplies. David had high aspirations for the temple, and every worker was given special training. They were told to be obedient to God. Being named people of God was a great honor.

During his life, David has done some horrible crimes. Every time David sinned, he would display complete and total repentance. He was always remorseful. He accepted the punishment he received from God without complaint. Wherever feasible, David made apologies and protected the innocent where he could. David had a desire to construct a house for God. The issue was that God had commanded him not to build the house for God. Solomon was permitted to construct it in the name of God. (1 Kings 8:17-20).

Following King David's death, his son Solomon was named king. Solomon was David's and Bathsheba's son. He was given instructions on how to complete God's temple. And David said to Solomon, "My son, I had planned to construct a house in the name Jehovah my God." But God spoke to me and said, "you have shed much blood and waged vast wars; you shalt not build a house on my name because you have spilled much blood upon the earth in my sight." (1 Chronicle 22:6-8). "And David said to Solomon his son, be strong and courageous, and accomplish it; fear not, nor be discouraged, for the God, even my God, will be with you; He will not fail you nor abandon you until all the work for the service of God's temple has been completed." (1 Chronicles 28:20.)

David died and was buried at David's City. He had ruled Israel for forty years, seven in Hebron and 33 in Jerusalem.

CONCLUSION

David Teaches Us Valuable Lessons.

The world around us is constantly changing. We are witnessing significant scientific and technological advancements accompanied by a sharp fall in moral standards. Christians must reject the world's anti-God spirit. However, as the world evolves, we change in many ways as well. We grow from childhood to adulthood. Wealth, health, and loved ones can all be gained or lost. Many of these changes are beyond our control, and they can pose new and formidable spiritual challenges.

Few persons went through a drastic life upheaval as David, the son of Jesse. David rose quickly from anonymity as a shepherd child to national legendary status. He then became a fugitive, pursued by a jealous king like an animal. David went on to become a king and conqueror. He had to suffer the repercussions of significant sin. He was the victim of tragedy and family strife. He accumulated wealth, became elderly, and suffered from the ailments of old age. Despite the multiple changes in his life, David maintained his faith in God and His spirit throughout his life. He did everything he could to portray himself to God as "approved," and God blessed him. (2 Timothy 2:15) Even though our circumstances are not the same as David's, we can learn from his approach to life. His example can show us how to continue to rely on God's spirit for guidance when we confront changes in our lives.

David's Humility Is An Excellent Example

David was not well-known as a child, even among his own family. David's father gave seven of his eight kids to the prophet Samuel when he came to Bethlehem. The sheep were entrusted to David, the youngest son. Nonetheless, God had chosen David to be Israel's future king. David was summoned from the field. "Samuel took the horn of oil and anointed him among his siblings," the Bible says. From that day onward, the spirit of God started to work upon David." (1 Samuel 16:12,13) Throughout his life, David relied on that spirit. This shepherd child would soon become famous across the country. He was summoned to serve the king and perform music for him. He slew Goliath, a giant so fearsome that even Israel's most experienced troops feared facing him. David, who was in charge of the army, defeated the Philistines. People adored him. They wrote songs in praise of him. An adviser to King Saul had previously hailed young David as "a valiant, great man and a man of war and an intelligent speaker and a well-formed man," in addition to being "excellent at playing" the harp. —1 Samuel 16:18; 17:23,24; 45:1;18:5-7.

David appeared to have it all: fame, good looks, youth, eloquence, musical abilities, military prowess, and heavenly favor. All of these things could have made him arrogant, but they didn't. Take note of David's response to King Saul's offer of his daughter in marriage. "Who am I and who are my kinsfolk, my father's line, in Israel, that I should become the king's son-in-law?" David said, humbly. (1 Samuel 18:18) David's statement here shows that neither on personal grounds, nor on account of his social standing, nor because of his family lineage, could he make the slightest pretension to the honor of being the king's son-in-law. David's humility stemmed from his understanding that in every manner, God is incomparably superior to fallible humans. David was astounded that God even notices man. (Psalm 144:3) David also understood that any success he had was due to God's humility in lowering himself to support, protect, and care for him. (Psalm 12:35)

What a wonderful lesson for us to learn! Our abilities, accomplishments, and advantages should never make us arrogant. We must acquire and maintain the humility to receive God's holy spirit and enjoy his favor. —James 4:6.

Do Not Seek Vengeance On Yourself.

While David's popularity did not inspire vanity in him, it did inspire homicidal jealousy in King Saul, who had lost God's spirit. Even though he had done nothing wrong, David fled for his life and took up residence in the wilderness. During one of King Saul's continuous pursuits of David, he entered a cave without realizing David and his men were hiding inside. David's men encouraged him to seize the supposedly divinely-ordained opportunity to kill Saul. "Here is the day on which God does say to you, 'Look!', I'm putting your enemy into your hands, and you must treat him as you deem appropriate.' —1 Samuel 24:2-6.

David was adamant about harming Saul. He was satisfied to leave things in the hands of God, exercising faith and patience. "May God judge between me and you," David replied when the king had left the cave, "and God must take vengeance on my behalf, but my hand will not come to be upon you." (1 Samuel 24:12). David did not seek vengeance, nor did he talk abusively to or about Saul, even knowing that he was wrong. David refrained from taking matters into his own hands-on countless other occasions. He instead trusted God to put things right. —1 Samuel 25:32-34; 26:10-11.

You, like David, may find yourself in difficult circumstances. Perhaps classmates, coworkers, family members, or others who do not share your beliefs oppose or persecute you. Retaliate in no way. Pray for God's holy spirit to come to your aid. Perhaps others who are skeptical will be inspired by your exemplary behavior and change. In any case, be rest assured that God is aware of your situation and will act in his own time.

Pay Attention To Discipline.

Years went by. David rose to prominence as a beloved king. His amazing faithfulness throughout his life, as well as the magnificent psalms he wrote in the worship of God, may easily give the idea that he would never commit a serious sin. He did, however, fall when he committed adultery. David accepted the discipline. He kept trusting in God's spirit. While God did not spare David from the wrath of his sin, he did forgive him.

All humans are imperfect. We, like David, may occasionally slip into major sin. God corrects people who wish to serve him in the same way that a loving parent corrects his children. Discipline is beneficial, but it is difficult to maintain. It can be "harsh" at times. (Hebrews 12:6,11) We can, however, reconcile with God if we "listen to discipline." (Proverb 8:33) To continue to receive God's spirit's blessings, we must accept correction and work to be approved by God.

www.ingramcontent.com/pod-product-compliance
Lightning Source LLC
Chambersburg PA
CBHW071921120726
48001CB00005B/1817